CW00342032

TEA

A DRINK WITH JAM AND BREAD

VICKY EDWARDS

summersdale

For Katie

With grateful thanks and much love for
tea-leaf reading, advice, laughter,
inspiration and wisdom.

About the author

Vicky Edwards is passionate about tea and averages eight cups a day. Working as an actress gave her the opportunity to gallivant around the UK on national tours, acquiring on her way an in-depth knowledge of some of the best teashops in the country. Since shelving her thespian aspirations she has juggled a career in press and media relations with freelance writing and broadcasting work. She lives in Sussex with her husband, their baby and a collection of teapots, cosies and sugar tongs.

Contents

BAGS OF HISTORY

There are several *stories* surrounding the *origins* of tea but the most popular is from Chinese *mythology* and dates back to sometime around 2737 BC…

ONCE UPON A TEATIME a Chinese emperor called Shen Nung was sitting under a shady tree, thinking imperial thoughts. Under the very same tree Shen's servant was boiling a pot of water in order that his master should have a purified drink with which to quench his thirst when he had finished his important pondering. Suddenly, a breeze ruffled the branches of the tree, causing a few leaves to flutter down and into the boiling water. Our man on pot duty made to fish out the offending leaves but was stopped by Shen Nung who, when he wasn't busy being an emperor, was a keen herbalist.

Recognising the tree as a wild tea tree, Shen wondered what the taste of this infusion might be. Leaving the leaf to brew awhile he then sampled the flavoured water and declared it to be refreshing and delicious. Thus, under that shady tree all those years ago, Shen Nung was responsible for concocting what is today the world's most popular drink.

By the time the third century AD rolled by, much had been written about tea and its beneficial properties. However, it wasn't until 618 AD when the Tang dynasty kicked in that tea (*ch'a*) achieved the grand status of becoming China's national beverage. Buddhist priests travelling around China and Japan were responsible for passing on not only religious enlightenment but also the delights of tea drinking.

By 850 AD the Arabs had got their hands on the great brew and it is they who claim to have introduced it to the thirsty Europeans. Not so, say the Portuguese and Dutch, who reckon that the introduction of tea to Europe was down to them. As early as 1515, priests on board Portuguese ships sailing to China to trade passed on the tea-drinking habit to the Portuguese sailors. These sailors convinced the Dutch of the benefits of tea and gradually the drink developed international appeal.

In 1610 consignments of tea began to arrive in Europe, but England was slow on the uptake. It was 1657 before Thomas Garraway became the first shopkeeper to sell tea. After suffering the horrors of the Great Plague of 1665, Londoners especially started drinking more tea, as it was clear that a drink made with boiling water was a safe beverage to enjoy. In the late seventeenth century, England signed up to trade through the East India Company, and teapots began to be imported into Europe from China in massive quantities. By the eighteenth century, tea and tea sets were something of a status symbol in England's aristocratic homes.

The British government imposed taxes on tea in Britain between 1689 and 1964 and also in the American colonies. This pleased nobody, not least American merchants who, in 1773, in protest against the charge that they had to pay, heaved a shipment of tea into the sea. This event went down in the history books as the Boston Tea Party and many patriotic Americans turned to coffee in protest. This may explain why our friends across the pond don't share the British passion for tea. Meanwhile, Britain's way of dealing with the unwelcome tax was to turn to smuggling and contraband tea became big business.

Until the nineteenth century, ships took up to fifteen months to make the journey from China to London. The advent of the tea clipper, a sleeker vessel that could carry more cargo, cut the journey time greatly. The most celebrated clipper was the *Cutty Sark*. Built in 1868 she actually only transported tea on a handful of voyages. The Clipper Races became a popular annual event. The race started in China, and the first ship to unload its cargo in London was declared the winner.

During the Industrial Revolution the workforce drank tea by the bucketful, which was provided by happy employers. Happy, because tea was non-alcoholic, cheap and, with milk and sugar added, made for an energy-giving drink that would keep the workers toiling for hours on end.

By 1900 there were thousands of tea estates in North and South India and in Sri Lanka. Much of the produce was bound for London auctions and Mincing Lane became known as the world centre of the tea trade. Rationing during the Second World War made tea a luxury item, but since then one of Britain's greatest traditions has been enjoyed by millions.

TEATIME TRIVIA

In June of 2004 it was announced
that the Yorkshire-based family firm
Taylors of Harrogate had won a contract
to export tea… to China! £30,000-worth
of the company's flavoured teas was said
to be winging its way to Shanghai,
including China Rose Petal. Ironically, its
leaves are grown and blended in China
and then sent to the UK for packaging.

TEATIME
INTERNATIONAL

TEA IS MANUFACTURED from the dried leaves of the *Camellia sinensis* plant. More than thirty countries produce tea, including India, where the rich soil of the valleys makes for perfect growing conditions. Soil is just one of the factors that influences the taste of tea. The time at which the leaves are picked and the way in which they are dried are also significant. But the biggest impact on flavour is down to climate. Tea grown at high altitudes has the most delicate flavours. Because of the differences in climates throughout the world, as well as the various means of blending, there are an estimated 1,500 teas to pick from.

For all the different *blends*, there are actually only three *types* of tea: black tea, green tea and oolong tea. A fusion of tea from two or more regions or estates, blended teas are usually a mix of different leaves that produce a unique flavour.

ASSAM IS A STRONG TEA THAT
COMES FROM THE HUMID
BRAHMAPUTRA VALLEY IN
INDIA. IT HAS A DELICIOUSLY
MALTY TASTE AND IS DEEP
BROWN/GOLD IN COLOUR.
IDEAL AT BREAKFAST TIME,
ESPECIALLY WITH A BIG FRY-UP.

GROWN IN THE HIMALAYAS, DARJEELING HAS A REPUTATION FOR BEING THE 'CHAMPAGNE OF TEAS'. THIS IS DUE TO ITS DELICIOUS, DRY TASTE. PERFECT FOR AFTERNOON TEA SERVED WITH TRIANGULAR SALMON OR CUCUMBER SANDWICHES.

EARL GREY IS A BLEND OF BLACK CHINA TEA SCENTED WITH OIL OF BERGAMOT. AN AFTERNOON TEATIME FAVOURITE IN THE UK, THIS DELICATE BREW IS BEST DRUNK WITH A SLICE OF LEMON. YOU ARE CONSIDERED A 'POSH' TEA DRINKER IF THIS IS YOUR BREW OF CHOICE!

LAPSANG SOUCHONG IS
THE BEST-KNOWN CHINA TEA.
AN UNUSUALLY SMOKY-
FLAVOURED TEA, ITS UNIQUE
TASTE IS A RESULT OF BEING
DRIED OVER PINEWOOD FIRES.

SERVED WEAK AND WITHOUT MILK, JASMINE IS A DELICATELY SCENTED CHINESE TEA AND A BRILLIANT PALATE CLEANSER. A SINGLE POT CAN BE TOPPED UP WITH HOT WATER SEVERAL TIMES WITHOUT COMPROMISING THE FLAVOUR.

JASMINE TEA WAS THE INSPIRATION FOR MANY OF THE **HERBAL** AND **FLAVOURED** TEAS THAT HAVE, OVER THE PAST TWENTY YEARS, GROWN IN POPULARITY. HOWEVER, THEY ARE NOT TEA IN THE ACCEPTED SENSE AS THEY DO NOT ORIGINATE FROM TEA PLANTS BUT FROM FRUITS, ROOTS AND HERBS.

THE SERIOUS TEA DRINKER
GENERALLY REGARDS THESE
TISANES WITH GREAT
SCEPTICISM. HOWEVER, A CUP
OF PEPPERMINT, PEACH OR
CAMOMILE TEA CAN BE A
REFRESHING DRINK TO
SOMEONE WHO IS EITHER
OBLIGED TO CUT BACK ON
CAFFEINE OR WHO JUST
FANCIES SOMETHING FRUITY.

TEATIME TRIVIA

Storing tea correctly is crucial to
preserving the flavour. An airtight canister
(not glass) with a snugly fitting lid is best.
Keep your tea caddy in a cool and dry
environment, away from strong odours,
as tea is prone to absorbing
other flavours.

MATTERS
MEDICAL

TEA HAS LONG BEEN KNOWN AS AN ESSENTIAL REMEDY.

Without milk, tea has no calories, so it is the ideal choice for dieters, and introductory trials suggest that green tea may influence weight loss by speeding up fat oxidation. Several cosmetic companies are now supplementing their skin care products with green tea extracts, as it is believed to be beneficial to the complexion. It is also thought to provide protection against certain cancers.

A cup of hot, sweet tea has been sworn by for generations as a vital antidote for shock.

Anyone who has ever given blood knows that a cuppa with added sugar is a great tonic, and in labour wards, new mothers see midwives as angels for bringing them a steaming cup of reviving loveliness after the trials of childbirth.

Raspberry leaf tea is said to help kick-start labour for expectant mothers who have passed their due date.

Tea contains fluid and antioxidants so drinking 3–4 cups a day (with milk) provides a variety of vitamins and minerals and also contributes to the body's hydration process.

According to a recent news report in the *Daily Mail*, drinking two cups of tea per day increases your life expectancy by up to four years.

TEATIME TRIVIA

The aristocracy brought about the traditional afternoon tea in England in the 1940s. The fashion then was to serve dinner at 8 p.m., which meant that the length of time between luncheon and dinner created embarrassing tummy rumblings. Ladies started to take tea and cakes in their boudoirs and it wasn't long before the idea caught on and drawing-room tea became customary in English society.

CHINA IN YOUR HAND

The **teapot** has come a long way since Shen Nung's original **experiment** but, remarkably, it was a good four thousand years before the Chinese **adapted** this rather simple method of brewing. A few basic amendments were made to the traditional Chinese wine ewer and thus the teapot as we recognise it today **evolved**.

POTTY FOR POTS

To own the perfect non-drip teapot is the dream of many an ardent tea drinker. If you are lucky enough to have such an item amongst your crockery, guard it with your life! It would seem that whatever the material, the teapot will inevitably develop a 'drip' habit at some point, even if it starts life behaving itself beautifully.

The type of teapot you select is a very personal choice. Some go for style over practicality and some have a preference for a particular shape. Some teapots are family heirlooms that are handed down the generations, and some pots are so well loved that they are welded together with glue and a prayer…

Classic Brown Betty teapots are made from red terracotta clay. Many believe that this classic chubby pot, with its Rockingham glaze, makes the perfect cuppa.

Silver teapots became highly popular in the 1700s due to their durability and because they retained the temperature of the tea so well. Silver pots today smack of top-drawer tea drinking, but are high maintenance on the cleaning front.

Glass teapots are ideal for those who like to monitor their brew and serve it only when it has attained a particular colour and density. They don't look so pretty on the tea tray, though.

Porcelain teapots are usually the most decorative, appealing to those who like a matching set – cups, saucers, plates, milk jugs – as these afford the best opportunity for collecting additional pieces.

PRESENTATION

When serving tea, remember: stainless steel is a no-no in upper-echelon tea circles.

Sugar should be of the cubed variety, served with tongs.

Fresh milk and hot water served in jugs to match the teapot should also be part of the final tableau, which should be presented on an elegant tray, with snowy white damask napkins and appropriate cutlery for any food that is also being served.

THE MUG V CUP DEBATE

This debate has been raging a long while. Some consider mugs to be the choice of workmen and believe that a cup and saucer is the only way to take tea. The counter-argument is that a mug makes no difference to the quality but sure as heck offers a better deal in terms of quantity. Whatever your preference, it is probably true to say that a cup or mug made from bone china will offer an altogether more enjoyable supping experience. But everyone should drink tea from a cup and saucer every once in a while, if only to help preserve tradition.

TEATIME TRIVIA

In Zambia a man divorced his wife —
even though it was he who had been
playing away. The wayward hubby
became hopping mad with his missus
after finding a frog in a cup of tea she
had made him. 'That is why I went with
another woman,' said the
two-timing tea drinker.

BREWING

THERE ARE SEVERAL POINTS TO BEAR IN MIND WHEN TRYING TO ACHIEVE THE PERFECT CUPPA.

Quality is everything in tea brewing so always use the best loose-leaf tea or tea bags that your budget can stretch to.

Fill the kettle with fresh cold water. If you live in a hard-water area then it is best to filter the water first and de-scale your kettle regularly. Stale water will affect the taste of the tea even after it has been boiled.

Warm the teapot with boiling water.

Add the tea. As a general rule of thumb use one rounded teaspoon of tea or one bag per person. You can amend this to suit personal taste.

As soon as the water boils, add it immediately to the teapot. Over-boiled water makes tea taste like old socks.

Let the tea steep. Small-leafed black tea generally needs 2–3 minutes but the larger-leafed black tea requires 3–5 minutes. In most instances manufacturers indicate a brewing time on the packaging.

If milk is to be added to the cup then this should be done *before* pouring the tea. This allows it to blend more smoothly with the tea.

TEATIME TRIVIA

In Japan in the late fifteenth century a
family had as many as twenty items for
the preparation of tea, and the cabinet in
which they kept these utensils was
regarded as a significant status symbol.
The first great Japanese tea-master,
Shuko, wrote rules for the handling of
the Japanese tea utensils.

THE LEAVES
TELL ALL

TEA-LEAF READING (tasseography), like the drink itself, is thought to date back to ancient China. It is also associated with Eastern European gypsies, and has roots in Scotland and Ireland.

The basic idea of tasseography is to identify the symbols in the cup and present a reading based on what shape the leaves take. Different symbols have different meanings and need to be carefully identified to ensure an accurate reading.

The cup should be presented to the reader only when the person has drunk a full cup of tea and drained the liquid. The reader looks with her 'third eye' at the patterns in the cup, allowing instinct to interpret the leaves.

- **Heart** – Love
- **Ladder** – Promotion
- **Man** – A visitor is heralded
- **Owl** – Gossip
- **Rabbit** – Bravery is required
- **Shoe** – Change for the better
- **Table** – Family harmony and jolly parties
- **Wasp** – Problems in matters of the heart

TEATIME TRIVIA

Tea played an important role in the
temperance movement. Tea meetings
were held all over the country in an effort
to convert drinkers and to raise money
for the movement's work. It is believed
that the phrase 'teetotal' may have
originated from these meetings.

Top of the Pots

The UK's finest teashops

The following suggestions are the personal recommendations of
the author and do not reflect any merit system.

BETTYS CAFÉ TEA ROOMS

6–8 St Helen's Square, York, North Yorkshire, YO1 8QP
Telephone: 01904 659142
www.bettysandtaylors.co.uk

First opened in 1919 and one of five 'Bettys' (also at Harrogate, Ilkley, Northallerton and York), this teatime success story is a glorious step back in time. In this refuge from the push and shove of modern living, you'll often hear live music courtesy of a discreet but talented pianist as you sample Bettys' famous tea and cakes. A speciality menu of Yorkshire and Swiss dishes is also on offer.

BIRD ON THE ROCK TEA ROOM

Abcott, Clungunford, Shropshire, SY7 0PX
Telephone: 01588 660631

This award-winning tea room not only boasts fabulous home-made food and an extensive selection of teas, including some unusual gems, but is staffed by a team who are as welcoming as hot buttered toast on a winter's morning. It has a charming quainty-dainty atmosphere and there is also an excellent selection of tea-related gifts to take away as mementoes of your visit.

OSBORNE HOUSE

Promenade, 17 North Parade, Llandudno, Conwy, LL30 2LP
Telephone: 01492 860330
www.osbornehouse.com

At this beautifully renovated Victorian hotel, tea is usually served in the lounge. The glorious interior decoration, including chandeliers and marble floors, provides the perfect backdrop for ladies who like to lunch or revel in a refined but delicious cream tea.

THE PUMP ROOM

Roman Baths, Stall Street, Bath, Somerset, BA1 1LZ
Telephone: 01225 477785
www.romanbaths.co.uk

Part of the original Roman Baths, lunch or tea in the splendid surroundings of the Pump Room is a must if you find yourself in this neck of the woods. Rich in atmosphere, this has been Bath's favourite meeting place since the eighteenth century. Highlights include live music – The Pump Room Trio or a solo pianist play daily – and the chance to try Bath's famous spa water from the fountain. Good and reasonably priced food and an excellent cuppa guaranteed.

THE RITZ HOTEL

150 Piccadilly, London, W1J 9BR
Telephone: 0207 4938181
www.theritzlondon.com

The ultimate in decadence, afternoon tea at The Ritz is one of the greatest of British traditions. Smart dress is essential (jackets and ties for chaps and definitely no jeans), as is a healthy bank account (set price for full tea will set you back £34 per person). However, an exceptional choice, delectable food and the sheer opulence of this venue ensures that you get your money's worth.

ST MARTIN'S TEA ROOMS

3 St Martin's Street, Chichester, West Sussex, PO19 1NP
Telephone: 01243 786715
www.organictearooms.co.uk

A rare treasure tucked away in the very heart of Chichester's bustling shopping area, this pretty Grade II listed building houses one of the country's finest tea rooms. As well as a splendid selection of tea, St Martin's offers healthy, home-made organic light meals and cakes. Open fires enhance winter visits and a charming garden offers tea alfresco in the summer.

CLARINDA'S TEA ROOM
69 Canongate, Edinburgh, Midlothian, EH8 8BS
Telephone: 0131 557 1888

Located in Edinburgh's trendy Royal Mile, one of the best things about Clarinda's Tea Room is having your tea leaves read. With an extensive menu, (their home-made scones are a scrumptious speciality) this tranquil tea-drinker's haven is well worth crossing the border for.

A must-see attraction for all fans of the
Big Brew, the Bramah Museum of Tea
and Coffee can be found at
40 Southwark Street, London.

Telephone: 0207 4035650
www.bramahmuseum.co.uk

Teatime
Recipes

Boozy and Buttery Winter Biscuits

Ingredients (makes 25 biscuits)

1 oz / 25 g castor sugar

4 oz / 100 g butter

3 tbsp sherry (sweet)

7 oz / 200 g plain flour

Instructions

Preheat the oven to 180°C, 350°F, Gas Mark 4 and lightly grease 2–3 baking sheets. Using a large bowl, cream together the sugar and butter until pale and smooth, gradually adding the sherry. Add the flour a spoonful at a time, stirring between each spoonful. Transfer the dough to a floured surface and roll out to $\frac{1}{2}$ in / 1 cm thickness. Cut into rounds and then transfer to the baking sheets.

Bake for 15–20 minutes. Cool on wire racks.

Serve with a robust tea in front of a roaring log fire.

Scrumptious Scones

Ingredients *(makes 8 scones)*

2 oz / 50 g sugar

4 fl oz / 120 ml milk

8 oz / 225 g self-raising flour

2 oz / 50 g butter (cut into small pieces)

Jam and butter or whipped cream to serve

Instructions

Preheat the oven to 220°C, 425°F, Gas Mark 7 and grease a baking sheet. Sift the flour and salt into a mixing bowl, add the butter and rub in until the mixture looks like fine breadcrumbs.

Stir in the sugar then add the milk, one tablespoon at a time, stirring well with a knife until the mixture begins to stick together. Using one hand, collect the mixture together and knead lightly to form a smooth, soft dough.

Turn the dough out onto a lightly floured surface, form into a round shape and roll out to $1\frac{1}{4}$ in / 3 cm thick then cut out 2 in / 5 cm rounds using a pastry cutter. Make sure you handle the dough as little as possible and don't roll it out too thinly. Place on the greased baking sheet and brush the tops with a drop of milk.

Bake towards the top of the oven for about 10 minutes, until golden and well risen. Cool on a wire rack.

Serve with Earl Grey and lashings of jam and cream.

Rock Buns

Ingredients (makes 10 buns)

8 oz / 200 g self-raising flour

4 oz / 100 g butter

3 oz / 75 g currants or raisins

Pinch of nutmeg

3 oz / 75 g sugar

1 egg, beaten

2 tbs milk

Pinch of salt

Preheat the oven to 220 °C, 425 °F, Gas Mark 7.

Mix the flour, nutmeg and salt together. Then rub the flour and butter together until they look like breadcrumbs. The next stage is to add the currants, sugar, egg and milk. The mixture should be fairly firm.

Grease a baking tray with some butter. Mould the mixture into small lumps and place on the baking tray. Bake for 20 minutes.

Victoria Sponge

Ingredients

6 oz / 150 g self-raising flour

6 oz / 150 g butter

4 oz / 100 g caster sugar

3 eggs, beaten

Jam

Pre-heat the oven to 200 °C, 400 °F, Gas Mark 6. Mix together the sugar and butter until they are smooth in texture. Gradually add the eggs to the mixture, then fold in the flour. Grease two 7 in / 17 cm baking tins and divide the mixture between the two tins. Bake in the oven for 20 minutes.

To see if the cake is cooked, stick a skewer in the centre of the sponge. If the skewer comes out clean, the cake is ready.

Turn the cakes out of the tins onto a wire rack. Once cooled, spread a layer of jam over one of the layers, sandwich the other one on top, and sprinkle with caster sugar.

Flapjacks

Ingredients (makes 16 bars)

8 oz / 225 g porridge oats
4 oz / 100 g butter
3 oz / 75 g sugar
4 tbsp golden syrup
Pinch of salt

Preheat the oven to 180 °C, 350 °F, Gas Mark 4.

Melt the butter in a large saucepan, then add the syrup and leave over a low heat for a couple of minutes. Remove from the heat and add the sugar, salt and oats. Mix thoroughly using a wooden spoon, making sure all the oats are covered with syrup.

Grease a shallow baking tray and evenly spoon in the mixture.

Cook for 20–30 minutes. After cooking, cut the flapjacks into bars before they cool.

TEA DRINKERS'
HOROSCOPES

ARIES

As the boldest sign of the zodiac, Aries is the most likely to experiment with exotic teas and probably has an extensive selection stashed away in the larder.

Known for having a fiery temperament, beware the ram whose tea is not served piping-hot and in a bone china cup.

Aries are especially fond of fondant fancies to accompany their afternoon tea.

TAURUS

Taureans are at-least-two-cups-per-boil-of-the-kettle merchants and so prefer a pot of tea to a single cup or mug.

Sensual beings, they are especially fond of teas that offer texture as well as taste, and the offer of a pot of tea and a slice of rich home-made fruitcake is a sure-fire way to put a twinkle in the eye of any bull.

Extremely well organised, Taurus can be relied upon to run the most impressive tea tent at any fête or jamboree.

GEMINI

Easily bored but first-class communicators, Gemini will order their own tea and cake but will expect to have a sip and a nibble of all that you have ordered too.

Tea suggests a social gathering to those born under the sign of the twins and they are very fond of tea dances and meeting friends in teashops for a good gossip.

A cake stand that boasts an extensive variety of cakes and sandwiches is the perfect teatime treat for Gemini.

CANCER

Crabs are big fans of tea, especially Lapsang Souchong, which they drink by the oceanful.

The most retiring sign of the zodiac, Cancer is partial to taking tea in solitary, devoting time that others would spend chatting to allow their taste buds to revel in the experience.

They prefer a savoury dish, such as egg and cress finger sandwiches, to go with their afternoon tea.

LEO

The biggest show-off of the teatime signs, Leo's tea set will be the most ornate and any tea that they provide will undoubtedly be the most calorific.

At a teashop lions will over-order wildly, unable to confine themselves to just the one pot and a single pastry. They will definitely want to be Mother and pour, and will insist on cocking their little finger when drinking.

Leos are partial to Kenyan tea, not least because the tips of the leaves retain a golden colour that reminds them of their own blonde beauty.

VIRGO

The sign that will invariably have the neatest tea tray, the best-polished spoons and the most symmetrical triangular sandwiches.

Efficient in almost everything, if taking tea with a Virgo you will always be assured of good first aid treatment if you suffer any hot tea burns or choking-on-crumbs incidents.

LIBRA

Caring, sharing and charming, Librans will always drink a balanced two cups of tea at any serving and eat an even number of their favourite biscuits (gingernuts).

Very fond of getting back to nature, Libra is the most likely sign to risk scalding their pink bits by drinking hot tea in the buff.

Scorpio

The sexiest sign of all, Scorpio is blessed with an extremely vivid imagination.

Generally speaking they prefer coffee, but if taking tea then it will almost certainly be a strong blend with a good body.

Scorpio likes to revel in the physical experience of tea drinking and so is partial to a good slurp and dunk. They will never be embarrassed to be caught smacking their lips in appreciation of a good brew.

Sagittarius

The eternal optimist of the tea signs, Sagi always has a half-full mug (preferably a delicate tea such as Jasmine).

They have an engaging, childlike curiosity, which at teatime can get them into bother as they are prone to lift the corners of sandwiches and poke their fingers into the fillings of cakes. This doesn't go down well at The Ritz.

Capricorn

Sticklers for tradition, Capricorn like their tea the good old-fashioned way. Woe betide anyone failing to cut the crusts off bread or serving tea that has been stewing too long in the pot. That said, they are adventurous and will always be amongst the first to try new tea-drinking experiences.

One of the most charismatic signs, their tea parties are extremely jolly affairs and invitations are much sought after.

AQUARIUS

Sociable and easy company, Aquarius is also the dottiest sign and is more likely to wear the tea cosy than to use it for the purpose it was intended.

They are also the most gifted tea-leaf readers of the zodiac and therefore prefer loose tea to bags.

Regular chatterboxes, they often have to drink cold tea as they have talked for so long that their brew has chilled completely.

TEA TALK

IF MAN HAS NO TEA IN HIM,
HE IS INCAPABLE OF
UNDERSTANDING TRUTH
AND BEAUTY.

JAPANESE PROVERB

I ALWAYS FEAR THAT CREATION
WILL EXPIRE BEFORE TEATIME.

SYDNEY SMITH

THE PERFECT TEMPERATURE FOR
TEA IS TWO DEGREES HOTTER
THAN JUST RIGHT.

TERRI GUILLEMETS

STRANGE HOW A TEAPOT CAN
REPRESENT AT THE SAME TIME
THE COMFORTS OF SOLITUDE
AND THE PLEASURES
OF COMPANY.

ANON

THERE IS NO TROUBLE SO GREAT
OR GRAVE THAT CANNOT BE
MUCH DIMINISHED BY A NICE
CUP OF TEA.

BERNARD-PAUL HEROUX

BREAD AND WATER CAN SO
EASILY BE TOAST AND TEA.

ANON

GREAT LOVE AFFAIRS START WITH
CHAMPAGNE AND END
WITH TISANE.

HONORÉ DE BALZAC

REMEMBER THE TEA KETTLE · IT IS
ALWAYS UP TO ITS NECK IN HOT
WATER, YET IT STILL SINGS!

ANON

NEVER TRUST A MAN WHO, WHEN
LEFT ALONE IN A ROOM WITH A
TEA COSY, DOESN'T TRY IT ON.

BILLY CONNOLLY

YOU CAN NEVER GET A CUP OF
TEA LARGE ENOUGH OR A BOOK
LONG ENOUGH TO SUIT ME.

C.S. LEWIS